Thanks to Dr Patricia Casaer and Dr Joyce Jansen.

Copyright © 2021 Clavis Publishing Inc., New York

Originally published as *De oogarts* in Belgium and the Netherlands by Clavis Uitgeverij, 2020
English translation from the Dutch by Clavis Publishing Inc., New York

Visit us on the Web at www.clavis-publishing.com.

Optometrists and What They Do written and illustrated by Liesbet Slegers

ISBN 978-1-60537-628-8

This book was printed in January 2021 at Nikara, M. R. Štefánika 858/25, 963 01 Krupina, Slovakia.

First Edition
10 9 8 7 6 5 4 3 2 1

Clavis Publishing supports the First Amendment and celebrates the right to read.

Optometrists
and What They Do
Liesbet Slegers

Clavis

NEW YORK

You've got two eyes to look with.

But there are children who can't see really well.

They blink all the time or may even have headaches.

That can be a problem, but it doesn't have to be.

You can have the optometrist check your eyes.

Your eyes (or one of them) may need help.

The optometrist examines them thoroughly

and then tells you what to do.

The optometrist is a doctor.

She wears ordinary clothes,

and sometimes a white doctor's coat.

She has a lot of instruments with which

she can examine and check your eyes.

(Take a look at the special little flashlight she uses.)

Does every eye function properly?

Do you squint sometimes?

Can you see everything clearly?

little flashlight

doctor's coat

ordinary clothes

You put your chin on the belt at the bottom and your forehead against the bar at the top. This way, you sit in the right position.

.... ticket

The optometrist has a number of **large instruments**. With one of those,
she does the first eye test. Afterwards, a ticket comes out of the instrument.
The numbers on that ticket tell the optometrist a lot about the eyes.
With another large instrument, the optometrist can look inside your eye.
This is the **slit lamp microscope** that enlarges the inside of your eye. Cool!
Smaller instruments are the **little flashlight**, the **toys** you have to follow
with your eye, and **special cards** testing your sight.
She also has a TV **screen** with pictures you have to identify.
For each visit, you sit in the **optometrist's chair**, which can be raised or lowered.
Sometimes, the optometrist puts a few **drops** from a little bottle in your eye.
Turn the page to see how all of this works!

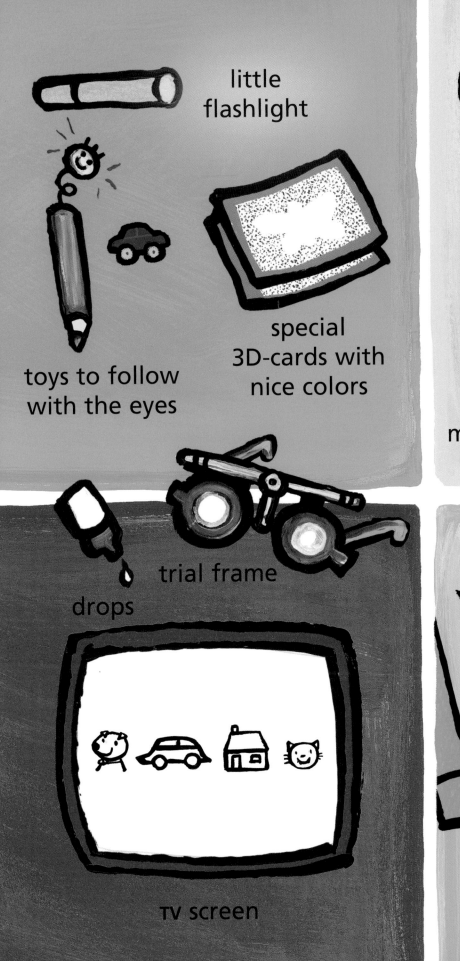

little flashlight

toys to follow with the eyes

special 3D-cards with nice colors

drops

trial frame

TV screen

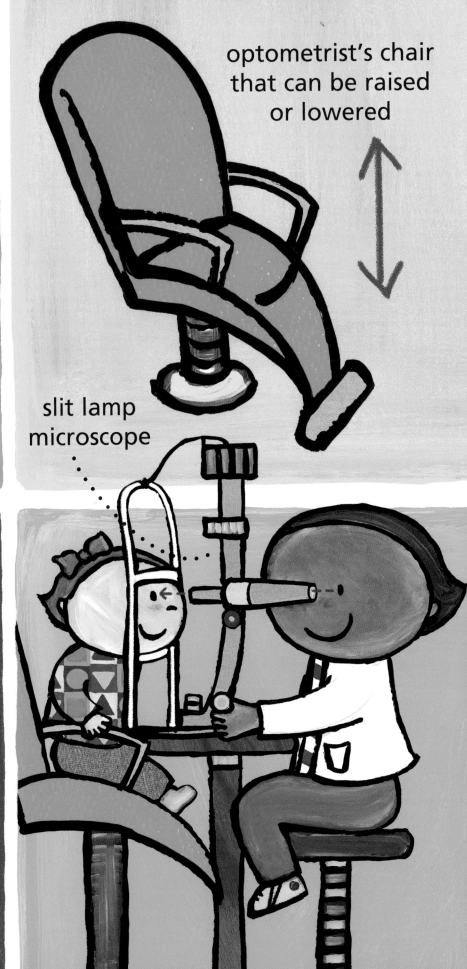

optometrist's chair that can be raised or lowered

slit lamp microscope

...... at the desk

"Hello Karen, this is your first visit to the optometrist, isn't it?
Have a seat over there," says the gentleman behind the desk.
Karen goes to the waiting room with her dad.
There are books and blocks to play with.
After a while, the optometrist is ready for them.
"Hi Karen," she says. "You and your dad can come with me now."

The optometrist examines the position of the eyes. She shines the little flashlight in Karen's eyes.

"You can go and sit comfortably on the big chair, Karen," the optometrist says.

Karen can sit on it on her own! Her dad gets another chair.

The optometrist pushes a button and the chair goes up. Wow, nice!

"Now we're going to do some tests," the optometrist says.

First, she looks into Karen's eyes with the little flashlight.

Can her eyes follow the light?

Next, the optometrist covers one eye at a time with her hand.

"This way, I can see whether or not an eye squints," the doctor says.

Then, she moves a little car sideways.

Are the little muscles of every eye strong enough to follow the car?

Now, Karen gets a funny pair of glasses, with one green lens and one red lens.
Without these glasses, Karen can only see the cross in the red frame.
But when she puts on the glasses, she suddenly sees the other forms
which are hidden between the dots!
"Can you point out where the triangle is? And where the little square is?"
the optometrist asks.
Wow, the optometrist has a lot of things to examine people's eyes!

The optometrist measures the eyes. This is done with a portable instrument, or at a table.

Karen looks with both eyes through an instrument

that the optometrist holds close to her face. She hears a nice tune.

"Which drawing do you see inside?" the optometrist asks.

"A flower!" Karen laughs.

Meanwhile, the optometrist looks into Karen's eyes

from the other side of the instrument.

Now, Karen is asked to look at the flower with one eye at a time.

The test is over. A ticket with numbers comes out of the instrument.

By now, the optometrist knows quite a lot about Karen's eyes.

The next test is Karen looking at pictures on a TV screen.

The optometrist swaps them with the remote control.

First, Karen looks at large drawings. She can see and identify those easily.

New pictures are shown and they become smaller and smaller.

Karen cannot see the smallest pictures very clearly.

But that's no problem. First, one eye is covered with a beautiful eye occlusor,

or a patch that covers the eye. Then the other.

This way, each eye can be examined separately.

The trial frame
with different lenses

"These are funny glasses!" Karen laughs. She can put those on too.

The optometrist has a drawer full of lenses.

In each side of the trial frame, she can choose a different lens.

She tries a number of them. Which lenses help Karen identify

the smallest pictures on the TV screen perfectly?

The eye drops sting a bit,
but not for long. Let's count to ten.
After that, the stinging will be gone.

Then, the optometrist puts a few drops from a little bottle in each of
Karen's eyes. "These drops will relax your eye muscles, so that I can
look at them even better," the optometrist says. "So, both of your
eyes will take a rest now."
It takes some time for the drops to work.
Therefore, Karen can go and play with the blocks. Nice!
Because of the drops, Karen can't see well at close range for a while,
but that's no problem.
"All right, Karen, you can come back now for the last tests!"
the optometrist says.

Advice from the optometrist
After your visit to the optometrist, the drops will keep working for some time. When the sun shines bright outside, you'd better wear a cap or sunglasses to protect your eyes.

After the optometrist has looked through the microscope, she repeats the test with the flower.

Karen returns to the big chair. Now, she can sit behind the largest, coolest instrument! She puts her chin on the belt and her forehead against the bar. This way, she sits right in the middle.

The optometrist watches each of Karen's eyes through the microscope.

A light shines into the eye that the optometrist looks at.

The doctor can now see the inside of the eye as well. Wow!

Meanwhile, Karen looks at the optometrist's ear.

That way, the doctor can examine her eye best.

After that, Karen is asked to look at the flower in the other instrument once again.

Now, the optometrist can measure whether Karen needs glasses. Exciting . . .

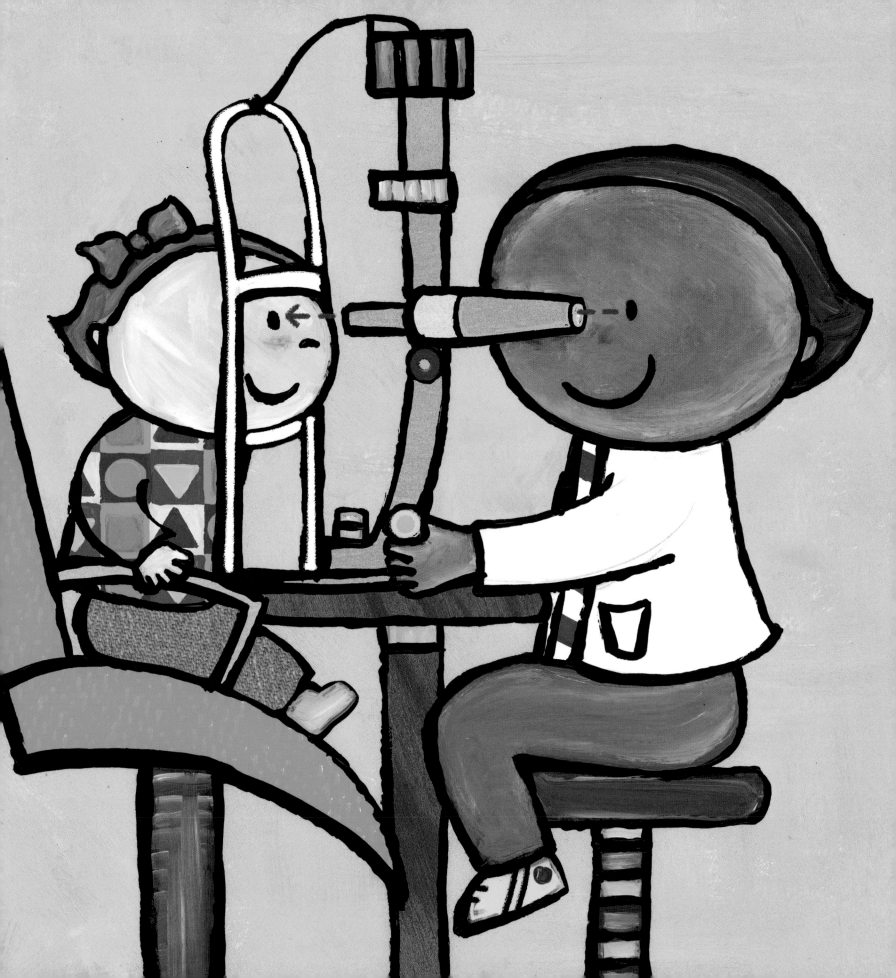

The eye occlusor covers the eye that sees well. This way, the other eye will learn to see better.

"That's it, we're ready. You did that very well, Karen!" the optometrist says. Karen is proud.

"In order to see the small pictures clearly too, you can go and choose a lovely pair of glasses at the optician. And now and then, you should cover your right eye with one of these cute eye occlusors. This way, your left eye will learn to see better. When you take off the occlusor, you can stick it on this lovely boat. That's fun, isn't it?"

Karen is a little bit tense, but above all, she's very glad.

With her new glasses, she'll see everything clearly!

"Bye, doctor," Karen says. "See you soon!

Next time I'll bring my boat full of eye occlusors."

The optometrist has another nice test. With this funny instrument,
one eye gets to see something the other eye doesn't.
One eye sees the fish, the other eye sees the fish bowl.
And what do both eyes see together? Right, the fish swimming in the bowl!
This instrument has a difficult name. It's called the synoptophore.
With it, the optometrist examines whether your eyes work well together,
or she measures how much the eyes squint.